Perspectives
Hazardous Adventures
At What Cost?

Series Consultant: Linda Hoyt

Flying Start
to Literacy®

Contents

Should adventurers put their lives at risk?

When adventurers take part in risk-taking sports or activities, they put themselves in danger. If they get into trouble and need rescuing, newspaper reports of the dramatic rescues attract public attention – and this often leads to fierce debate.

Should adventurers expect to be rescued if they get lost or injure themselves? Why should rescuers put their own lives at risk to rescue people who choose to put themselves in dangerous situations? Rescues cost a lot of money. Who should pay for them? Is it more than a question of money?

Dangerous rescues – who pays?

When news stories about adventurers trapped in dangerous situations hit our screens and newspapers, our first thoughts are for the people in trouble and how to save them.

In this article, Claire Halliday explains that these rescue missions are not only dangerous, but also costly.
So, who should pay?

Dramatic rescues

Active, adventurous people can find themselves in dangerous situations. Some might be lost explorers stuck on snow-covered mountains, or unlucky sailors floating in the ocean after their boat has capsized. Hikers who take a wrong turn onto an isolated desert track, without enough precious water, can also need rescuing.

The stories of their rescues are exciting ones and the happy endings are thanks to search and rescue professionals. But the nature of these rescue missions raises an important question. Who should pay for the cost of the rescue?

The cost of danger

Search and rescue operations can be expensive. Helicopters, boats and specially trained rescuers need to be paid for. Other emergency service specialists, including police, fire crews and ambulance officers, also cost money. Who does pay?

In many parts of the world, the people who need to be rescued are not asked to cover the costs of their rescue. Instead, public donations and government assistance cover the expense of the rescue mission. However, in some countries, the person or people being rescued are expected to pay the bill.

This is not the case in Canada, where search and rescue experts have regular calls from mountain resorts. Snowboarders and skiers are frequently trapped in difficult weather conditions. Often, people become lost or injured after they have left official paths and trails, but they can still expect to be rescued.

Many people believe that big rescue bills should be covered by the government and taxpayers for safety reasons. Some rescue experts worry that if people stop calling professional rescue teams to avoid a big bill, they might get into worse trouble. It may help to spend money on better education to teach adventurous travellers to be prepared with water, food, safety equipment and the right technology to call for help and show their location.

Money vs. doing what is right

Whether or not to save the people at risk is never the issue. After all, when people are in trouble, helping them is always the right thing to do. But for adventurers who choose to put themselves at risk, the debate about who should pay the rescue bill continues.

Adventurer rescued after four days at sea

Solo around-the-world yacht races can be dangerous for sailors and costly for rescuers. Ellen Morris recalls the story of stricken sailor Tony Bullimore, whose amazing rescue cost millions of dollars.

Should sailors be encouraged to take such risks? Are they heroes? Or are they irresponsible thrill seekers?

The cost of rescue

On 5 January 1997, British sailor Tony Bullimore's yacht became stranded in the Southern Ocean, during a solo around-the-world race. The yacht had lost its keel in the rough conditions and capsized. Trapped in the upturned yacht, and with water pouring in, Bullimore was in serious trouble.

He managed to find shelter in an air pocket in the upside-down boat where he rigged up a hammock to keep himself above the water. The 57-year-old adventurer had lost all his food supplies and had only one bar of chocolate to eat.

The Royal Australian Navy launched a mission to rescue the sailor and, on 9 January, after surviving four days at sea, Bullimore heard rescuers banging loudly on the hull of his yacht and shouting his name. The rescuers were amazed to find him alive.

Tony Bullimore

HMAS Adelaide in the Southern Ocean, where Tony Bullimore's yacht capsized. Rescue boats were launched from HMAS Adelaide.

Altogether, the Royal Australian Navy was involved in the rescue of three sailors during the race: Bullimore, Thierry Dubois and Raphael Dinelli. The combined cost of all three rescues was more than ten million dollars.

Questions were raised about the risky routes the rescued sailors took and the costs of the rescues. The Australian Maritime Safety Authority's search and rescue operations manager, Rick Burleigh, said the southerly routes the sailors took were a dangerous shortcut.

"Down in those waters, there is more wind, so they go faster and they also have to travel a shorter distance. But the conditions are much more dangerous and they are much further from help if they do get into trouble."

The Australian government argued against any criticism about rescue costs. A spokesperson for the government said that the experience gained by search and rescue experts in the difficult conditions was something money could not buy.

He also said that rescues were an international legal obligation. "We have a moral obligation, obviously, to go and rescue people, whether in fires, cyclones or at sea," said the spokesperson.

Are robots better explorers than humans?

Deep-sea exploration is dangerous. In this article, journalist Kathryn Hulick argues that robots are better suited to exploring the deepest parts of the ocean because the risk to human explorers is too great.

What do you think? Should people continue to explore the deep ocean? Or should we send robots?

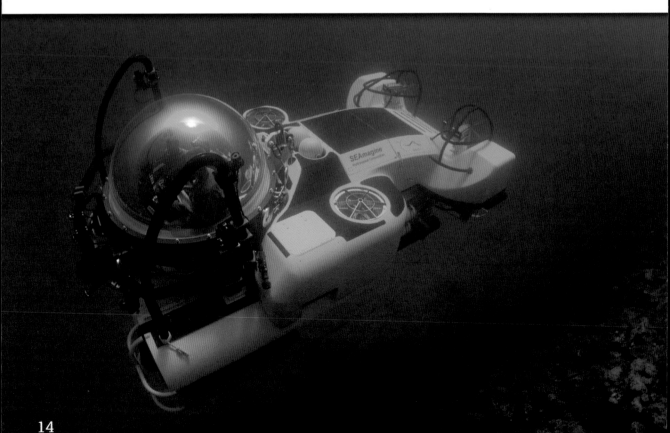

Vast stretches of land beneath the ocean remain shrouded in mystery. In 2012, movie director and explorer James Cameron, having spent ten million dollars of his own money, made history when he became the first person to travel alone to the deepest place on Earth: the Challenger Deep, 11,000 metres under the Pacific Ocean.

But does it really make sense for people to visit the sea floor? Today, only eight vehicles exist that can carry people 2000 metres under the sea. By comparison, approximately 10,000 robots are out there exploring the deep sea. (Mining and drilling companies operate most of them.)

James Cameron (inset) and the submersible craft, the *Deepsea Challenger*

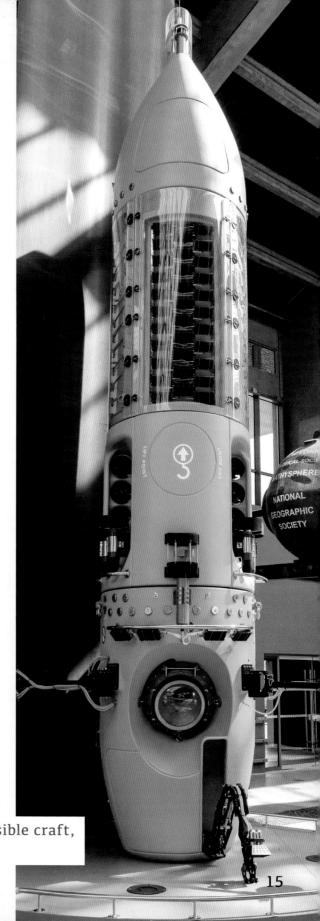

15

Human explorers need to breathe, eat, drink and sleep. They also have to dive and return to the surface very slowly and carefully to adjust to changes in pressure. Without a special vehicle, a human would be squashed like a bug under the weight of all that water.

Robotic submarines can explore extreme locations safely, without putting human lives in danger. They can also dive faster and stay under the water longer than a person. All they need is a boat to launch from and a source of power. Engineers at the surface watch the video feed from the robot's cameras and help control where it travels. They can even instruct a robot to pick up rocks, sea creatures or pieces of shipwrecks.

A robot inspects a sunken ship deep under water.

Humans are still better than robots at looking around underwater and deciding when to snap a photo, what to collect or where to go next while exploring. But, as computer technology improves, robots are getting smart enough to make some of these decisions on their own.

No matter how smart robots get, though, people such as James Cameron will want to experience the thrill of venturing into the unknown. Can a person still feel that rush while controlling a robot from afar? Is the excitement of discovery worth risking human lives in the dangerous, deepest parts of the ocean?

Taking risks

People who enjoy adventures in remote, wild places often experience a great sense of personal freedom and achievement. Many people, however, believe such thrill seekers take pointless risks, when there are lots of other ways to have fun.

Do you agree with any of the people quoted in this article?

When I dive into the deep ocean, I get a huge rush of adrenalin. There are risks, but I train hard and feel well prepared for any difficulties I might encounter. Besides, life has many other dangers.

I love being outdoors. When I reach the mountain's summit, there are breathtaking views of nature. Training for a climb makes me feel healthy and strong.

When I go caving, I know I am taking great risks. I try to be careful. If I get into trouble, I don't expect other people to risk their lives to save me.

Some rescue operations cost millions of dollars. The money used on these rescues would be better spent on charities that benefit larger numbers of people.

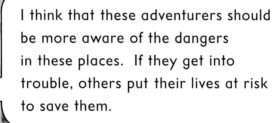

I think that these adventurers should be more aware of the dangers in these places. If they get into trouble, others put their lives at risk to save them.

There are so many other things that people can do for enjoyment, without the costs or dangers involved.

19

Rescuers risk lives to save dog

In this article, Claire Halliday writes about the dangers for rescuers in hazardous situations. They often put their own lives at risk to save others. In this report about the rescue of Mary, the beagle, she asks whether rescuers should risk their lives for animals.

What do you think? What is an animal's life worth?

Dangerous rescues

Have you ever found yourself in a dangerous situation and needed help? Maybe you climbed up a tree in the park and felt too scared to climb back down by yourself. Maybe you went skiing and got stuck on a hill that was too steep. Every day, all around the world, people find themselves in trouble. It could be because of an accident, dangerous weather conditions, or they might have been taking a risk, just for fun. When people are stuck in dangerous situations, they often need someone else to help them get to safety. But often rescuers put their own lives at risk to save someone else.

The rescue of a pet beagle

People are not the only ones who need rescuing. In the snowy mountain region of Utah in the United States, a pet beagle became stranded on a steep, icy ledge. When its owner called for assistance, a team of search and rescue specialists, who were volunteers with the Utah County Search and Rescue, came to help.

Animals are difficult to rescue. Because they are already feeling frightened, the sight of strangers trying to get close to them can scare them even more – and they often try to get further away, which makes the rescue even harder. That's what happened with Mary, the beagle.

The rescuers worked in very slippery, cold conditions, which put their own lives in danger. The dog was frightened and would not move. "I realised that if I got any closer to that dog, and tried to grab her collar, it might upset her," said Mr Shaun Roundy, one of the Utah County Search and Rescue volunteers. "And I was afraid she was going to jump right off the edge of the cliff. Her feet were just right there at the edge."

Eventually, the crew made the decision to give up for the night.

Mr Roundy left Mary some food for the night, including a can of sardines, a pack of beef jerky (dried meat) and a muesli bar. The rescue team also left a bag with some hand warmers, to give Mary a warm place to sit in the freezing temperatures.

Should the team have stayed? Should humans risk their lives to save animals?

Mary gets home safely

The crew were happy to try again the next day. But, to everyone's astonishment, Mary somehow found her own way and climbed down from the icy ledge. She arrived home with just a few cuts and scratches. Her owners were thrilled to have their pet safe and thankful for the efforts of the search and rescue team.

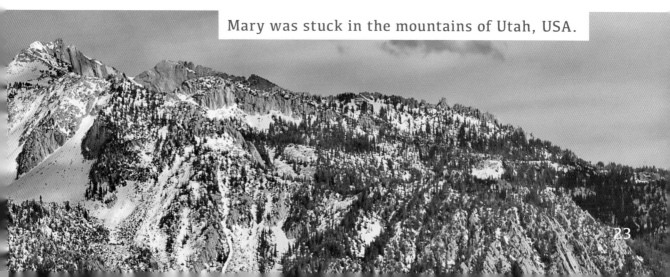

Mary was stuck in the mountains of Utah, USA.

What is your opinion? How to write a persuasive argument

1. State your opinion

Think about the issues related to your topic. What is your opinion?

2. Research

Research the information you need to support your opinion.

Related PERSPECTIVES book   Internet   Other sources

3. Make a plan

Introduction
How will you "hook" the reader?
State your opinion.

List reasons to support your opinion.
What persuasive devices will you use?

Reason 1
Support your reason
with evidence and details.

Reason 2
Support your reason
with evidence and details.

Reason 3
Support your reason
with evidence and details.

Conclusion
Restate your opinion. Leave your reader with a strong message.

4. Publish

Publish your persuasive argument.
Use visuals to reinforce your opinion.